LET'S JUST LAUGH AT THAT
FOR KIDS!

BOOK TWO

STEVE BACKLUND

with Brendon Russell, Janine Mason, Julie Heth, Melissa Amato, & Sally Schwendenmann

Let's Just Laugh At That For Kids, Book Two
© copyright 2017 Steve Backlund, Igniting Hope Ministries
ignitinghope.com
E-mail: info@ignitinghope.com

Cover illustration: Scott Burroughs
Cover design: Robert Schwendenmann
Interior layout and formatting: Robert Schwendenmann

Author picture photography: Tracey Hedge
Contributing authors: Steve Backlund, Brendon Russell, Janine Mason, Julie Heth, Melissa Amato, Sally Schwendenmann
Editor: Melissa Amato
Special thanks to: Chris Pollasch, Megan Cotton, Marcia Russell, Ryter family

ISBN-10: 0-9863094-9-4
ISBN-13: 978-0-9863094-9-6

Unless otherwise noted, all Scripture quotations are taken from the Holy Bible, New Living Translation, copyright ©1996, 2004, 2007, 2013 by Tyndale House Foundation. Used by permission of Tyndale House Publishers, Inc., Carol Stream, Illinois 60188. All rights reserved.

Please note that the author's publishing style capitalizes certain pronouns in Scripture that refer to Father, Son, and Holy Spirit and may differ from other publishers' styles.

LET'S JUST LAUGH AT THAT

BOOK TWO

LAUGH AT THAT

FOR KIDS!

TABLE OF CONTENTS

INTRODUCTION

APPENDIX

LIES   PAGE

ABOUT THE TEAM

STEVE BACKLUND

Steve is on staff at Bethel Church in Redding, CA. He and his wife Wendy founded Igniting Hope Ministries and travel extensively, equipping the body of Christ with hope, joy, and victorious mindsets. He is a contagious laugher, skilled in the art of destroying bad beliefs.

BRENDON RUSSELL

Brendon, a father of four, has spent many years serving in children's ministry. As a child, Brendon did not tolerate boredom well. It is his passion to make the Word of God as interesting and applicable as possible to help kids realize how fun and caring God is. He has greatly benefited himself from the concepts taught in this book.

JANINE MASON

Janine is someone who is passionate to see every child develop into everything that they are designed to be. With four children of her own, she has a passion for education and has spearheaded "Kingdom in the Classroom" initiatives at Bethel Church including workshops and conferences for educators.

JULIE HETH

Julie was so impacted by the message of hope and joy as an intern under Steve that she stayed on another year as Project Manager for Igniting Hope Ministries where she contributed to *LJLAT For Kids, Help! I'm A Pastor*, and the facilitation of online and local events. She now resides in Chicago where she works for a major non-profit organization serving over 1,000 kids in under-resourced communities, helping them to have new and abundant lives.

MELISSA AMATO

Melissa has experience working with children in various capacities. She was a Pediatric ER nurse, a preschool teacher, taught performing and fine arts to kids, led children's ministry, and much more. She lives to love and is passionate about seeing people of all ages walk in the abundant life Jesus paid for. Melissa is on staff in BSSM as the Third Year Student and Mentor Pastor.

SALLY SCHWENDENMANN

Sally is currently a stay-at-home Mom and loving it! As a former teacher for 11 years, she is passionate for children to live in full truth and abundance. She attended all three years of BSSM where she was blessed to meet and marry her husband. She is currently working on other projects to bring Jesus to the nations.

DEAR KIDS,

YOU CAN BE THE STAR OF YOUR LIFE!

Every good story has the star and a bad guy. In our life story, we get to be the star and overcome the bad guy. The bad guys are not people who seem to be out to get us. The bad guys are lies we believe! When we believe lies, we settle for less than God's best. To be the best we can be, we need to destroy these lies and believe the truth about who God says we are. When we agree with God on something, we become unstoppable, but it will take some time and work. To become the star of our own life story, we must become fantastic lie detectives who sniff out lies that hold us back from the destiny God has for us.

The Bible makes it clear that we have an enemy (Satan) who is called the father of lies (John 8:44). He is scared of the power we have and tries his best to take us down, but he has no power except the ability to tell us lies. He tries to get us to believe false things about ourselves, others, and God.

Lies seem true inside our heads. One of the enemy's strategies against us is to make us think we are alone – that we are the only one who feels or thinks the way we do, and that things will never change. If we keep lies hidden, they're harder to get rid of. When we bring them into the open, we see them for what they are – stinky lies trying to stop us from getting to our destinies.

Psalm 2:4 says that God sits in the heavens and laughs. What is He laughing at? He is laughing at the enemy's plans and lies to destroy us. God knows the enemy doesn't have any real power, so He does not worry about his lies. Instead, He laughs at them.

In this book we will learn to laugh with God at the lies that come against us to hold us back. We will use our laughter as a weapon against lies. The weapons in this book that are fueled by your laughter include: the Laughter Blaster, the Laugh-achine Gun, the Giggle Grenade, the Ha Ha Hammer, and the Laughter Boots.

When we laugh at lies, we start destroying the power they have. As the lies in our mind start to crumble, we then finish defeating the enemy by replacing the lies with the truths of God. In this book, we help you do that through verses from the Bible, declarations to speak, and practical activities to help you remember and know truth at a deep level.

Learning to destroy lies is pretty easy once we know how, but it doesn't happen all at once – it is a journey as we change what we believe a little at a time. It is like building a house. This looks really hard at first, but when we put down one brick at a time, we begin to see walls form. Before we know it, the house is complete! This is how it is with overcoming lies and believing truth. We can change the way we believe by dealing with one lie at a time. And we don't have to be perfect in the process. If we mess up and believe a lie again, we don't have to be discouraged. Failing doesn't make us a failure, it simply means we are learning to change the way we think.

WE KNOW YOU CAN DO IT!
YOU ARE A STAR!

DEAR PARENTS,

Picture what your life would have been like if, as a child, you hadn't believed any lies about yourself. Imagine if your insecurities weren't there about the way you looked or how smart or talented you were. Imagine if fear had no power because you disarmed it with the truth about how God sees you. Imagine if you had always believed God is good and He delights in you. Take a moment and really let it play out in your mind. I would bet that you are sensing a greater freedom and joy than the reality of your childhood. Truth brings freedom and joy.

Many of us, as adults, still struggle to come to terms with the truth about ourselves, God, and the others around us. Our vision is to see a generation of young people walk in truth from an early age, knowing who they are and who their God is. It is possible, and it starts with us.

No matter how you define success, everyone wants it for the young people in their lives. We desire for them to have successful relationships with God and others, a successful education, and a successful career. Our hope for them is that they thrive and become the best version of themselves in every area of life. Our role in their lives now, and in preparing them for their future, cannot be underestimated. The Bible says to train a child in the way they should go, and when they are old they will not depart from it (Proverbs 22:6). We have a responsibility to set them up for success by training them and giving them tools to have good beliefs.

Each one of us lives out of what we truly believe. We're not talking about what we think we believe at a head level, but we are talking about what we really believe at a deep down heart level. Kids are no different. They react to the world around them and make decisions based on what they believe about themselves, others, and God. We see their outward responses and are sometimes mystified by their reactions, but we often fail to recognize that their actions come from an internal belief that is opposed to truth.

This book is designed to be a tool for us to help teach the important children in our lives how to deal with the lies coming against them. These lies, if left unchecked, will rob them of their destiny and of thriving in life.

We believe it is possible to create an environment where it is normal to expose lies for what they are and to walk in truth. God's design is that children everywhere are trained in not just what to think and do, but also what to believe. Our dream is that our places of influence become places where it is normal to talk about what we believe, the lies we are facing, and the truth of God's Word.

We pray that as you read this book, radical breakthrough will come for you and your children. We dream of healthy families who will speak the truth to one another in love, and walk in tremendous joy because of it. We declare lies that have held kids captive will be exposed and neutralized as you laugh together. We declare that "Nothing is impossible!" will become your normal experience as a family. We release new levels of connection and freedom into your household that will affect not only your house, but also your whole neighborhood. We declare the kids you love will become a part of a new generation that takes God at His Word, believes the truth, and does amazing exploits in the earth.

BLESSINGS,
Steve, Brendon, Janine, Julie, Melissa, and Sally

HOW TO GET THE MOST OUT OF THIS BOOK

KNOW THAT YOU ARE BUILDING A CULTURE

This book is more than just another devotional to do with our kids. Instead, it is a tool to help us build a culture of truth and good beliefs. Changing the culture in our houses or classrooms is going to take a bigger commitment than just doing a devotional.

To make the most of this book, we encourage you to get involved with your kids. Do the activities and make declarations together. Look for opportunities to continue discussing what you have been learning together without making it heavy. Keep fun at the center of what could otherwise be a heavy topic, and laugh together often.

IMMERSE YOURSELF IN THIS BOOK IN THESE WAYS

- Read it straight through with your children to get saturated with the truth.
- Read it with your children as the different lies come up.
- Read it together. Pick one lie a week, memorize the scripture, make declarations during the week, and complete each action step.
- Read it with a group of children, and activate them in speaking truth and completing the action steps in creative ways.

TRUTHS TO UNDERSTAND THIS BOOK

GOD LAUGHS (PSALM 2:4)

What is God laughing at in this Psalm? He is chuckling at what His enemies are saying and planning. We can become more like God by laughing with Him at the ridiculousness of Satan's lies. The phrase "Let's Just Laugh at That" has the unusual ability to remove power from the enemy's lies and prepare our hearts for the truth. We have adapted these truths for children with the idea of our laughter arming a weapon with power to destroy lies. This enables us to have a visual picture of what is happening in the spirit realm as we laugh at lies instead of choosing to believe them.

THE BATTLE IS BETWEEN TRUTH AND LIES

John 8:32 tells us truth will make us free. The Kingdom of God is not moved forward primarily by good behavior, but by good beliefs. In working with children, we often focus on their behavior instead of their beliefs. However, if we teach them to have good beliefs, behavior will follow. We can teach a child how they should behave, but they will remain spiritually weak if they are believing lies. In each chapter, we share truths to believe in place of the lie. Knowing truth will build a foundation of good beliefs.

KNOWING TRUTH BRINGS HOPE

Hope is what allows us to keep walking when we don't understand and positions us to step into faith. When we are believing truth, our hope level will be high. We can recognize if we are believing truth or lies by our hope level. We can increase our hope level by increasing our knowledge of God's truth. We will grow in hope as we grow good beliefs.

BRIGHT FUTURES COME FROM PRESENT GOOD BELIEFS

Romans 12:2 gives us an invitation into supernatural living. It says, "Let God transform you into a new person by changing the way you think." We transform our tomorrow by transforming our minds today. Intentionally renewing our minds with truth is a skill set that is vital for our children to learn to reach their full potential. We must not think, "Lord, tell me what to do," but rather, "Lord, tell me what to believe." Our children will be set up for success when we train them how to renew their minds, recognize lies, and believe truth.

WE HAVE TO LET GO OF SOMETHING IN ORDER TO LAUGH

To truly laugh at lies, we have to let go of some things including bitterness, hurt, and unbelief. Children laugh more frequently than adults. This may be because they have lived fewer years and have less to let go of. When we teach children to laugh at lies when they are young, we can be confident they will use this skill far into their adult years. Learning to laugh at lies, instead of believing them, will prevent them from unnecessary hurt in the future. It is important to note: to be able to laugh at lies with our children, we have to remember that their current situation is not an indicator of our overall success as parents and teachers.

WALK IN LOVE AND WISDOM AS YOU LIVE A JOY-FILLED LIFE

We are to "Be happy with those who are happy and weep with those who weep" (Romans 12:15). We need to be sensitive to where children are at, and to what is going on in their lives as we seek to walk with them in increasing joy. Kids may really be having a hard time with the lies coming at them, and their circumstances may also be difficult. The tools in this book are to be used generously, but not apart from other tools like forgiveness, empathetic listening, clear communication, interactive discussions, and more.

WHAT IS IN EACH CHAPTER

THE PRIMARY LIE TO LAUGH AT / THE TITLE

This is a "kingpin" lie. You may hear it come out of your child's mouth, or you may see the effects of it through how they are behaving. We urge you to read the lie out loud and laugh audibly. Something powerful happens when the lie is brought into the light through speaking it out loud.

THE STORY

Each chapter includes a short story that children may resonate with. Read it through with emotion, and consider discussing if they have ever felt the way described.

MORE LIES TO DEAL WITH

This is a list of other lies that are commonly connected to the kingpin lie. This helps kids identify more lies they could be believing. It will also help you, as a parent or leader, find the root of the lie. After reading the additional lies, we encourage you to ask kids what else they are believing in this area. This is a wonderful opportunity to guide them to ask the Holy Spirit to expose other lies.

THE TRUTH

We cannot simply get rid of a lie; we must replace it with the truth. In this section, biblical examples and promises are provided to refute the lies. We encourage you to read the Bible stories mentioned with your kids to get the truth lodged in their hearts.

WHAT CAN I SAY?

Romans 10:17 says faith comes by hearing. A key way to renew our minds is to declare the truth out loud. Remember that Jesus did not think His way out of the wilderness, but He spoke truth to counteract challenges concerning His identity and the nature of His Father (Matthew 4:1-11). Declarations will help our children do the same. We recommend you work with your children to make declarations a normal part of life. Find fun ways of doing them together, and help them make the connection when change is linked to the declarations they have been making. Look for opportunities daily to speak declarations over your children and with them.

WHAT CAN I DO?

This section provides three helpful steps to reinforce truth in the area the lie addresses. Your involvement with this section is the key to it being successful. We encourage you to not only provide the tools for them to do the activity, but also to take the time to invest in following up with them on how it went. Remember, you are helping them learn a new way of believing that will set them up for success.

MY ATTITUDE DOESN'T AFFECT OTHERS

It's the end of a horrible day. You had the worst substitute teacher, and your best friend said you were a loser when you missed the final shot at today's basketball game. "I hate this day," you think to yourself. Now you're in the car with your family and your sister won't stop laughing and talking. You get annoyed and loudly sigh as you hunch down in your seat. "No one understands what I've been through," you think. "If they did, they would understand why I'm grumpy. My attitude is my business, and it doesn't affect anyone else." Suddenly you realize the car is quiet and your mom's smile has vanished. "Wait a minute. Did my attitude do this? Does my grumpiness affect other people?" You suddenly see the lie that was coming at you. You lob a Giggle Grenade at it and watch it explode!

LET'S LOB A GIGGLE GRENADE AT THESE LIES!

IT'S OKAY TO HAVE A BAD ATTITUDE IF I HAVE A GOOD REASON.

MY ATTITUDE DOESN'T AFFECT THE ATMOSPHERE AND OTHER PEOPLE AROUND ME.

A BAD ATTITUDE IS SOMETHING THAT HAPPENS TO ME, NOT SOMETHING I CHOOSE.

THERE IS NO REASON TO KEEP A POSITIVE ATTITUDE.

MY ATTITUDE IS MY BUSINESS AND NO ONE ELSE'S.

THE TRUTH

KEY VERSE

Proverbs 17:22

"A cheerful heart is good medicine, but a broken spirit saps a person's strength."

You may have heard adults in your life say, "Attitude is everything." Maybe you thought they were exaggerating and decided not to listen, but the truth is that your attitude tends to affect everyone around you. When you choose to respond to a bad day, a hard circumstance, or a grumpy feeling with a bad attitude, it's as if you are releasing a stinky gas into your environment. Pretty soon the people around you (unless they work hard not to be affected) are left coughing and gasping for air.

The Bible has a lot to say about our attitudes. Paul had many reasons to have a bad attitude but chose to be content no matter what (Philippians 4:11-12). We're called to be salt and light. We are carriers of hope and peace, and we are told in the Bible that we can wear Jesus and take Him with us (Romans 13:14). How we live our life shows others what God is like: loving, patient, and full of peace. When you choose a bad attitude, you cause the people around you to encounter negative things instead of encountering the positive and powerful God inside of you. You can choose to have a positive attitude and release good things wherever you go.

WHAT CAN I SAY?

- My positive attitude makes a difference.
- I can choose a good attitude.
- I influence people for good.
- My life shows other people God's love.

WHAT CAN I DO?

- **Choose who you want to be** - Keeping a good attitude, no matter what you experience, is a choice. Having a good attitude comes from focusing on who you are instead of what happened. Even if something bad happened, you are still a child of God who can look and act and think like Him. Make declarations to remind yourself of who you are. "Do everything without complaining and arguing ..." (Philippians 2:14).

- **Make a plan** - Sometimes you may react with a bad attitude because you don't have a plan. There are likely some things that usually upset you. Make a decision about how you will respond before one of these things happens again. For example, "When someone teases me, I'm going to tell them quietly how it makes me feel and then choose to forgive." Put your plan into action and change your behavior. "Good planning and hard work lead to prosperity ..." (Proverbs 21:5).

- **Use your imagination** - Next time you feel like having a bad attitude, spend a minute imagining toxic green gas coming out of your body and swirling around the people near you. Then imagine the golden glory of God being released from your body, carrying peace, love, and kindness to those people. Draw a picture now of these two different responses to help you remember what is happening when you choose your attitude. "So we don't look at the troubles we can see now; rather, we fix our gaze on things that cannot be seen" (2 Corinthians 4:18).

GOD DOESN'T WORK POWERFULLY THROUGH MY PRAYERS

It's Sunday morning and you watch as adults pray for people and amazing things happen. You think to yourself, "I wish I could be like them. When I pray, I don't even know what to say!" You get so embarrassed when you have to pray out loud that the words come out all mixed up, and you can hardly understand yourself. You get jealous as you hear other people pray so beautifully, and you comfort yourself with the thought that you will probably pray well when you are an adult. "After all," you think, "God doesn't work powerfully when kids pray." Wait a minute - who told you that? You just spotted a lie! Where's your Ha Ha Hammer? It's time to smash that lie!

LET'S SMASH THESE LIES WITH THE HA HA HAMMER!

I HAVE TO USE ALL THE RIGHT WORDS FOR MY PRAYERS TO BE EFFECTIVE.

GOD ONLY USES ADULTS TO HEAL PEOPLE AND TO DO MIRACLES.

ADULTS HAVE MORE FAITH AND ARE BETTER AT SPIRITUAL THINGS.

BECAUSE I FEEL AFRAID TO PRAY, GOD WILL NOT USE MY PRAYERS.

IF I DON'T FEEL POWERFUL, I'M NOT POWERFUL.

HA! HA! HA! HA! HA!

THE TRUTH

Some of the most mighty people who minister in God's power are under the age of twelve. Throughout history, God has used kids to heal people, encourage people, prophesy to people, and show them God's love. Check out the Bible for the stories of David as a shepherd boy slaying Goliath (1 Samuel 17), Josiah the King who was only eight years old (2 Kings 22), and the boy who fed 5,000 people with his lunch (John 6:8-13). Jesus loves children and loves to work powerfully through them.

In Mark 10, people were trying to bring their kids to Jesus. The disciples were sending them away, but the Bible says that Jesus was greatly displeased. He told the disciples why He wanted to be with kids. He said, "Let the children come to Me. Don't stop them! For the Kingdom of God belongs to those who are like these children ..." (Mark 10:14). Jesus recognizes that kids know how to have faith that is bigger than many adults. It's simply about believing Him. God uses people who believe in Him to do miracles, and kids are experts at believing. You may feel scared as you try new things (adults sometimes do too, even if they don't show it), but God always does something when you pray.

KEY VERSE

James 5:17

"Elijah was as human as we are, and yet when he prayed earnestly that no rain would fall, none fell for three and a half years!"

8

WHAT CAN I SAY?

- God's miracle-working power lives in me.
- My prayers are powerful to change people's lives.
- The size of God in me is more important than how big I am.
- Every time I pray, something happens.

WHAT CAN I DO?

- **Develop your relationship with God** - God loves to team up with His friends. The more you get to know Him, the easier it is to hear His voice and respond when He talks to you. Get to know Him more by spending time with Him, reading the Bible, praying, and worshiping Him. "Then He (Jesus) appointed twelve of them ... They were to accompany Him ..." (Mark 3:14).

- **Imagine God moving through you** - Spend time imagining yourself the way God sees you. Have you always wanted to see someone healed? Imagine God using you to heal someone. Do you want to pray and see your family get money to pay the bills? Imagine what it will be like when God responds to your prayer. "Fix your thoughts on what is true, and honorable, and right, and pure, and lovely, and admirable. Think about things that are excellent and worthy of praise" (Philippians 4:8).

- **Look for opportunities to try** - When we believe God, it's called faith, and faith pleases God. Look for people who need to be healed and ask them if you can pray. If they don't get healed the first time, don't be discouraged. You are growing your faith, and you just pleased God! Keep at it and you will see more and more good things happen. "They (believers) will be able to place their hands on the sick, and they will be healed" (Mark 16:18).

MY FEELINGS NEVER LIE TO ME

You wake up one Monday morning with the thought that your best friend has abandoned you and found a new best friend. You have been replaced! The more you think about it, the more convinced you become that your best friend is no longer your friend at all, but is spreading nasty rumors about you around school. As you arrive at school, you see your friend coming over to you. A thousand thoughts flood your mind and you feel tears come to your eyes. Your friend announces with a big smile, "I have a fantastic surprise for you." "A surprise?" you think, in shock. "Wait a minute, it felt so real that my best friend didn't like me. Could it be that my feelings lied to me?" It's time for a *Power Play*. Choose any laughter weapon to take that lie down!

IF IT FEELS TRUE, IT IS TRUE.

MY FEELINGS ARE ALWAYS BASED ON TRUTH.

MY FEELINGS KNOW BETTER THAN GOD ABOUT WHAT IS GOING ON.

I HAVE TO LISTEN TO AND ACT ON MY FEELINGS.

THE TRUTH

KEY
VERSE

Romans 12:2

"... let God
transform you
into a new
person by
changing the
way you think.
Then you will
learn to know
God's will for
you, which
is good and
pleasing and
perfect."

Did you know God has feelings? We are made in His image, and He gave us the ability to feel things in our hearts. Some of these feelings are good. At times we feel love or peace or excitement. Some feelings don't feel so good, but are okay for us to experience. It's normal to feel sad when a pet or friend dies, or to feel mad when someone hurts us. The trouble is that sometimes we have feelings that aren't true. Sometimes we can feel like God doesn't love us or that He is far away. It might feel so true at the time, but those feelings are lying to us.

Our feelings aren't the things that decide what is true. God's Word is the ultimate truth-teller. Everything that doesn't line up with what the Bible says is a lie. When we are feeling something and don't know if it's the truth or not, we can look at God's Word. Do you feel alone? His Word says He will neither fail you nor abandon you (Deuteronomy 31:6). Do you feel unloved? His Word says that He loved you so much that He sent Jesus to die on the cross for you (John 3:16). Do you feel like you can't do something? His Word says that nothing is impossible (Matthew 19:26).

WHAT CAN I SAY?

- I choose to listen to God's truth.
- God's Word and the Holy Spirit lead my life, not my feelings.
- I am filled with hope for every situation.
- When I believe truth, my feelings will catch up.

WHAT CAN I DO?

- **Value the Word of God -** God's Word is the truth. It has help for you with everything you are facing. When you are feeling sad, mad, or alone, you need truth to help you feel better. Write down your favorite Bible truths and keep them in a special box. Look at them when you need to know the truth. "Jesus said to the people who believed in Him, 'You are truly My disciples if you remain faithful to My teachings'" (John 8:31).

- **Learn to ask questions first -** When your feelings are trying to push you to respond to something before you actually know what is going on, stop and ask questions. Take a minute to find out from a friend or family member what they are thinking or feeling toward you. Asking questions helps lead to the truth. "Cry out for insight, and ask for understanding" (Proverbs 2:3).

- **Ask Jesus for help -** Was there a time when you were upset over something that ended up not being true? Think about how it would have been different if you listened to Jesus and not your feelings. Learn to stop and ask Jesus if your feelings are lying to you. Make a poster or pocket-sized card with a stop sign that says: When I have negative feelings, I STOP and ask Jesus if my feelings are lying to me. "Keep on asking, and you will receive what you ask for. Keep on seeking, and you will find. Keep on knocking, and the door will be opened to you" (Matthew 7:7).

I CAN'T DO IT

Sweat begins to drip down your forehead, and your palms get wet as you get closer to the front of the line. It's time to do something new in gym class, and you keep trying to think of a reason you need to go see the school nurse so you can get out of it. "It's so easy for all the other kids. Every time they try something new, they can do it so well. I wish I was like them. I wish things weren't so hard for me." These thoughts and others fill your head. Soon you hear, "I can't do it!" repeatedly within your head. Wait a minute! Who told you that? You suddenly realize this is just a lie, and it's time for it to be gone forever. You pull out your Laugh-achine gun and blast that lie into oblivion!

LET'S **BLAST** THESE LIES ALONG WITH THAT ONE!

IF I'VE NEVER DONE IT BEFORE, I CAN'T DO IT NOW.

THERE IS NO POINT IN EVEN TRYING.

I CAN'T DO NEW THINGS.

IF I DON'T GET IT RIGHT THE FIRST TIME, I WILL NEVER BE ABLE TO DO IT.

HA! HA! HA! HA!
HA! HA!
HA!

THE TRUTH

Have you ever heard the story of Jesus and Peter walking on water? Jesus was walking on water, and Peter stepped out of the boat and walked to Jesus (Matthew 14:28-32). Even disciples like Peter had to try new things they hadn't done before.

Peter began to sink when he took his eyes off Jesus, and Jesus brought him safely back to the boat. Peter was courageous because he at least stepped out of the boat. He may not have gotten it right his first time, but by taking that step of faith and trying something new, he was successful. Sometimes when we try something new, we do it well right away. Other times we may try and try, and still not be great at it.

Of course, we need to remember to be wise and not do everything we think of (like jumping off something high and trying to fly), but we still need to boldly try new things. Jesus is the one who called Peter to walk on water, which made it safe for him to try. Be courageous when Jesus calls. Those who think they can and those who think they can't are both right. Believe you can.

KEY VERSE

Philippians 4:13

"For I can do everything through Christ, who gives me strength."

WHAT CAN I SAY?

- I love trying new things.
- Even when I don't do things perfectly, I try again.
- I can do all things through Christ who strengthens me.
- I won't give up.

WHAT CAN I DO?

- **Try new things -** Everyone who has ever done anything great in life had to do it for a first time. You will too. Remember, your past doesn't decide your future. Build your confidence by trying new things and stepping out. Remember that it can take a lot of tries before we do something well. Set a goal to try two new things this week. "(Peter) walked on the water toward Jesus" (Matthew 14:29).

- **Celebrate with loved ones -** Celebrate your progress, not just perfection. Talk to your parents and ask them to help you celebrate when you try something you've never done before (even if you don't do it well at first). You can ask them for ideas about how to celebrate, such as having a family game night, singing a celebratory song, or letting you pick which movie to watch. "... encourage one another ..." (Hebrews 10:25).

- **Get a green light -** Every time you hear the words "I can't" enter your mind, ask the Holy Spirit if it's something you can and should do. Remember to use wisdom, and ask a parent or another adult you trust if you're not sure about something. If you get a green light (which means *go*) from God and an adult, say "I can" out loud, and go for it. "For I can do everything through Christ, who gives me strength" (Philippians 4:13).

I DON'T NEED TO TAKE CARE OF MY THINGS

You're done riding your bike, and you think about putting it away in the garage where it belongs, but it's so much easier to just leave it in the grass. You decide you'll put it away later. You go inside and play with some toys for a while and leave them on the floor when you're done. As you're getting ready to watch some TV and then go to bed, you realize you forgot to put your bike away and haven't cleaned up your toys yet. "It's okay," you think. "It doesn't matter if I put them away. I don't need to take care of my things." But then the thought that this might not be true comes to you, and you realize this is a lie. Throw the Laughter Boots on and stomp that tricky little lie!!!

LET'S **STOMP** THESE LIES TOO!

GOD DOESN'T CARE IF I TAKE CARE OF MY THINGS OR NOT.

IF SOMEONE ELSE TAKES CARE OF IT FOR ME LATER, THEN IT'S OKAY.

I ONLY HAVE TO CARE FOR BIG OR REALLY VALUABLE THINGS.

IT DOESN'T MATTER IF I TAKE CARE OF THINGS.

IT IS OTHER PEOPLE'S JOB TO PICK UP MY THINGS.

HA! HA! HA! HA! HA! HA! HA!

THE TRUTH

"The master
said, 'Well
done, my good
and faithful
servant. You
have been
faithful in
handling this
small amount,
so now I will
give you
many more
responsibilities.
Let's celebrate
together!'"

Luke 19:11-26 is a story of a man who became a king, and had given his servants some money to take care of him. The ones who were trustworthy and faithful with what they were given received a big reward - cities to take care of! The servant who didn't make good choices with the little he had ended up with nothing (and even the little he had was taken away).

Being faithful with little (even when it comes to things like toys) can lead to gaining more. Imagine sharing a toy with your friend. If they break it, are you happy to share another toy with them? Probably not. If they take care of it, you would be more likely to share more toys.

God wants to trust us with big things as we grow up. In the Bible story about the king, people who started with only coins and used them well were later trusted with cities. Like those in the story who gained more, we need to do our part and take care of what we have right now in order for us to learn faithfulness. Another part of taking care of what we have is being thankful for it. The more you practice being thankful, the more you will grow in faithfulness and being trustworthy.

WHAT CAN I SAY?

- I take great care of what I've been given.
- I am faithful when I have little and when I have much.
- I always choose to keep a grateful attitude.
- I pick up after myself and keep my room clean.

WHAT CAN I DO?

- **Be faithful now -** Take care of the things you do have. Keep your toys clean, play with them carefully (unless they were made for you to play hard with, like a football), and put them away when you're finished playing with them. This is being faithful in little things and it will help you have big opportunities in the future. "If you are faithful in little things, you will be faithful in large ones" (Luke 16:10).

- **Be inspired -** Read Bible stories of people who started with little, were faithful with what they had, and eventually were given a lot. Some of these people are Esther, David, Ruth, and Joseph. It can help to remember you are not alone, and knowing that others have been where you are and have overcome can help build your faith and hope. "So let's not get tired of doing what is good. At just the right time we will reap a harvest of blessing if we don't give up" (Galatians 6:9).

- **Give thanks -** Start a Thankful journal. Write down 1-3 things you are thankful to God for every day. They can be simple things like a beautiful flower, a smile from a friend, or having a good lunch. When you're feeling like you don't have much, read through your Thankful journal and remember what God has already done for you and given to you. "Be thankful in all circumstances, for this is God's will for you who belong to Christ Jesus" (1 Thessalonians 5:18).

THE FUTURE DOESN'T MATTER

HA! HA! HA! HA! HA! HA!

"Homework, shmomework," you think. You sit at the table with your forehead pressed against your math book. "Argh," you moan. "All I want to do is go and have some fun. How is this homework going to help me anyway?" You can't see why it matters, but your teacher keeps talking about your future. Future job, future family, future dreams … future, future, future! Frustration builds up inside you, and then you blurt it out: "I'm a kid, and I should be having fun now! I don't need to think about the future!" Hold on. You suddenly realize that doesn't sound quite right - it's a lie and it's time to get rid of it. Grab the Laughter Blaster and laugh this lie into vapor!

LET'S VAPORIZE THESE LIES TOO!

HOW I ACT NOW DOESN'T MAKE ANY DIFFERENCE TO MY FUTURE.

BEING CARELESS NOW WON'T MATTER LATER.

HAVING FUN IS ALL THAT MATTERS.

IF I'M NOT INTERESTED IN IT, IT'S PROBABLY NOT IMPORTANT.

THE TRUTH

Do you remember Noah from the Bible? God told him to build an ark (a very large boat). It took him one hundred years to do it. If Noah had not looked to the future and worked hard to create the ark, no one would have survived the flood that covered the earth (Genesis 5:32-10:1).

What would you like to be when you're older? Maybe you dream of being a police officer, a writer, a builder, a doctor, a website developer, a pastor, or a farmer. Any of these things will require training, practice, studying, and a determined attitude.

Having a great attitude now by being positive, hardworking, and kind, will set you up for an amazing future. In the Bible, whenever communities of people were looking to choose their leader, they would look for a person who was full of integrity and who loved God and worked hard. When we choose to work hard now and care well for what God has given us, it will always set us up for promotion and positive outcomes in the end. God, and others, do see your efforts.

KEY VERSE

Galatians 6:7b

"You will always harvest what you plant."

24

WHAT CAN I SAY?

- I am building for my future.
- I am setting myself up for great opportunities.
- I choose to do the hard things, and I know it's worth it.
- I do things now that lead to success.

WHAT CAN I DO?

- **Be thoughtful about your actions and words** - What you say and do does make a difference in your future and in the future of others. Get into the habit of pausing before you act or talk so you can think about whether it will be helpful or harmful. "You must all be quick to listen, slow to speak, and slow to get angry" (James 1:19).

- **Dream about your future** - What would you like to do in the future? Write a list and find an adult to share this list with. Talk to them about the different skills and training you would need to do these things. Discover what you can do now to help you reach your dreams. You can even open a savings account and begin to invest in that dream. "No eye has seen, no ear has heard, and no mind has imagined what God has prepared for those who love Him" (1 Corinthians 2:9).

- **Learn skills for the future** - Your family is a great place for learning things like being polite, trustworthy, and helpful. You can do chores with a great attitude and feel good about completing a job. If you learn these things when you are young, you will be given many more opportunities as you get older. You can learn skills now for jobs or ministry you will do in the future (like public speaking, writing, computer science, carpentry, etc.). "Do you see any truly competent workers? They will serve kings" (Proverbs 22:29).

MY FAMILY HOLDS ME BACK

You're lying in bed thinking about your friends and how their lives compare to yours. "Gary's dad is a doctor, Jill's parents are rich and have an amazing house with a pool, and Jack's dad is really fun and plays sports with him." Your thoughts then turn to your own family. They don't do and have the same things as other families. You wonder, "How am I supposed to be amazing with a family like mine? My family holds me back from having a good life." Uh oh! Can you smell it? That's a stinking lie. Pound that stinker to pieces with the Ha Ha Hammer!

LET'S POUND THESE LIES TO PIECES!

BECAUSE MY FAMILY ISN'T PERFECT, I WON'T HAVE A GOOD LIFE.

I WOULD BE BETTER OFF WITHOUT MY FAMILY.

I CAN'T DO ANYTHING GREAT BECAUSE OF MY FAMILY.

NOBODY WITH AN IMPERFECT FAMILY HAS DONE ANYTHING GREAT.

I'M GOING TO BE JUST LIKE MY FAMILY.

HA! HA! HA! HA! HA!

THE TRUTH

The truth is you are in God's family. He gives you a new bloodline and calls you His child. As a good Dad, He gives you access to everything His family has. The more time you spend with Him, the more you begin to look, think, and act like Him.

There are some characters in the Bible who came from what may have been seen as unsuccessful families. Ruth was a young widow who actually had no family of her own. Because she was faithful, God gave Ruth an amazing husband named Boaz. Several kings, including King David, are in her family tree (see the book of Ruth). Joseph's eleven brothers rejected him and sold him into slavery. Joseph later became the second in command of all of Egypt! He then invited his family to Egypt and honored them by giving them a place to live with him (Genesis chapters 37 and 39-47). Just like God had great plans for Ruth and Joseph even though their families had some flaws, He has great plans for you too!

KEY VERSE

Deuteronomy 5:16

"Honor your father and mother, as the Lord your God commanded you. Then you will live a long, full life in the land the Lord your God is giving you."

WHAT CAN I SAY?

- I am in God's family, and I am destined for greatness!
- Nothing can hold me back.
- I love my family for who they are.
- I will help my family get stronger.

WHAT CAN I DO?

- **Value and love your family** - Because you love God, you get to honor people no matter what they do. One way to help your heart and mind truly honor other people is to find ways to serve them, choose to learn positive things from them, speak positively about them, and encourage them. "His preaching will turn the hearts of fathers to their children, and the hearts of children to their fathers," (Malachi 4:6).

- **See your family likeness** - You are a child of God's and you look like Him. Have a friend trace your outline with chalk on the ground. Mark your hands as "hands that heal." Draw your mind as "a mind for wisdom." Draw a big heart and label it "a heart to love." With a teacher or parent, think of other things that are true about being in God's family, and mark them on your picture. "See how very much our Father loves us, for He calls us His children, and that is what we are!" (1 John 3:1).

- **Pave a trail** - If you want something, you will have to work for it. Often big dreams require trying new things that others aren't doing. Think of what you need to do to make your dreams come true. It might be studying to get good grades or working to make money. Every time you do these things, picture it as creating a trail toward your dreams in life. "... I focus on this one thing: Forgetting the past and looking forward to what lies ahead ..." (Philippians 3:13).

GOD WON'T PROTECT ME

Wow! You just broke your leg right before the youth ski trip. Why in the world did that happen? And last month when it was raining and you were trying to hurry to class, you slipped and fell, resulting in a painful arm injury that's still healing. You start to remember other times when you were hurt or when other people you love had accidents. You hear a shout in your head: "Oh no! God won't protect me!" Thankfully you come to your senses and remember that accidents and violence do happen, but God's heart is to protect you. You realize a lie has crept in your ear, and it's time to put on your Laughter Boots. *Stomp, stomp!* That nasty lie didn't stand a chance.

LET'S STOMP THESE LIES UNDER OUR FEET!

GOD ISN'T AWARE OF WHAT'S GOING ON IN MY LIFE.

HE LETS BAD THINGS HAPPEN TO TEACH ME LESSONS.

GOD IS TOO BUSY WITH MORE SERIOUS PROBLEMS.

GOD ISN'T POWERFUL ENOUGH TO PROTECT ME OR THOSE I LOVE.

BAD THINGS HAPPEN ANYWAYS, SO I DON'T NEED TO CARE ABOUT GOD.

THE TRUTH

KEY VERSE

John 10:28

"I give them eternal life, and they will never perish. No one can snatch them away from Me …"

Although life can be hard sometimes, God is always there for us. Psalm 91 says God will rescue us, protect us, and shelter us. Verse 11 says He will order His angels to protect us wherever we go. In Judges chapter 6, a man named Gideon was hiding because he was scared, and God sent an angel to help Gideon. Gideon didn't believe in himself, and the angel helped him see who he was in God's eyes (a mighty man of valor). It's awesome that God assigns angels to help us and protect us!

He also sent His only Son, Jesus, to help us and to save us. He sent the Holy Spirit to be our Helper and to help take care of us in the rough times. Protection is a big deal to God. It's such a big deal that He made a foolproof protection plan to get everyone into Heaven and live there with Him forever if they want to!

* Parents, read Steve's book *Divine Strategies for Increase* or *Cracks in the Foundation* for more biblical insight on God's protection

WHAT CAN I SAY?

- God protects my every step.
- God is always with me, and He will never leave me.
- He sent His Son, His Spirit, and His angels to protect me!
- As I grow in God, I will see fewer accidents in my life.

WHAT CAN I DO?

- **Memorize scripture about God's protection** - God's Word talks a lot about His protection. Make a fun game with family and friends to see who can find and memorize the most scriptures about God's protection. The more scriptures you find, the more you'll believe the truth. And the more you believe it, the more you will experience it. "I have hidden Your Word in my heart …" (Psalm 119:11).

- **Focus on protection** - Make a list of ways in which God has protected you. Ask others how God has protected them in different situations, and keep a record of it. Remember that every day you live, He has protected you from harm. You can be thankful for God's protection against things like fear, insecurity, and shame as well, not just physical situations. "This I declare about the Lord: He alone is my refuge, my place of safety" (Psalm 91:2).

- **Talk about God's promises** - You will see more of whatever you talk about a lot. If you always talk about problems, you will see more problems in your life. If you talk a lot about God's promises, such as protection, you will see more of that in your life. Start talking more and more about God's promises. The "What Can I Say?" section of each chapter in this book is a great way to start. "The tongue can bring death or life …" (Proverbs 18:21).

I DON'T HAVE TO HONOR MY BROTHER OR SISTER

You are lying on your bed, playing your favorite game. *Thump.* Your brother has just come in and jumped on you. "Get off me," you say. He continues to bounce five or six more times, then leaps off, pushing his feet into your back as he goes. Blood rushes to your head in rage, "What's wrong with you?!" you scream. Feelings of anger start to take over your brain, and in that moment you can't see a single thing you like about him. Words start to form in your mind: "I can't stand my brother! He's such a pest! I don't need to be nice anymore!" Stop right there! It's a good thing you can quickly grab your Laugh-achine Gun and destroy that icky lie!

HA HA HA DESTROY THESE LIES TOO!

I SHOULDN'T HAVE TO HONOR SOMEONE SO ANNOYING.

BROTHERS AND SISTERS ARE TO BE ENDURED, NOT ENJOYED.

PEOPLE ONLY DESERVE MY RESPECT WHEN THEY TREAT ME WELL.

I CAN TREAT THEM HOWEVER I WANT BECAUSE WE ARE STUCK WITH EACH OTHER.

THE TRUTH

Everyone who has lived with a brother or sister does not have a choice about it. There are times when they are in your face and seem just plain annoying. Unlike other people in your life, you get to see everything about them - the good, the bad, and the ugly. And you know what? They get to see all these things about you too. And that is something good to remember.

Even though we might not always agree or always get along with someone, we still need to see them as God does. God made everyone in His image, so when we honor or recognize the value God places on a person, we honor God. We are His precious children, and that does not change depending on how people behave.

Jesus told us to love one another (John 13:34-35). He did not say to love people only when they are really nice. (Remember, there are no perfect people except for God.) Part of growing up is learning to look past the annoying things people do and love them for who they are. Family gives us a great place to practice that.

WHAT CAN I SAY?

- I was created to honor everyone.
- I am learning to love people for who they are.
- I can control how I respond to my brothers and sisters.
- Every day, I grow in love for my family.

WHAT CAN I DO?

- **Celebrate your brothers and sisters** - Get a photo of your brother or sister. Glue it to a piece of cardboard that is larger than the picture. Write all the things they are good at around the picture on the cardboard, then draw arrows from the words to the picture. Also write what you appreciate about them or nice things they have done for you. If you get stuck, ask God how He sees them. "We always thank God for all of you and pray for you constantly" (1 Thessalonians 1:2).

- **Do random acts of kindness for them** - Be deliberate in showing that you want to love and live in peace with your brother or sister. Every day give them a kind word, do a kind act, or do both of these. Put a piece of candy on top of their pillow, write a nice note, or play their favorite game with them. "Love never fails" (1 Corinthians 13:8, NKJV).

- **Practice how you will treat them ahead of time** - Prepare ahead of time to respond with love to any situation. Think of the things that usually upset you (for example, your brother enters your room or your sister takes your toy and she often breaks things), and then think of how you would like to respond with loving words rather than negative ones. Repeat these loving phrases before a situation happens. Prepare yourself to speak how you want. "Commit everything you do to the Lord. Trust Him, and He will help you" (Psalm 37:5).

MY TEACHER DOES NOT LIKE ME

You are just minding your own business in class, and the teacher suddenly calls your name. "Oh no, not again," you think. "Here I was minding my own business and the teacher has to pick on me." Not knowing how to answer the teacher's question, you feel embarrassed and can sense your classmates staring at you. You think about how you aren't your teacher's favorite, in fact you're fairly sure she doesn't like you at all. Thoughts of anger begin to rise up in you. "Why does the teacher always pick on me? This teacher doesn't like me, so I won't like her either. I'm not even going to talk to her!" Stop right there! You take a Giggle Grenade out of your pocket, pull the pin, and explode these lies!

EXPLODE THESE LIES TOO! BYE BYE LIES!

MY TEACHER HATES ME.

I AM NOT SMART ENOUGH TO BE LIKED.

MY TEACHER WANTS ME TO FAIL.

I CAN NEVER DO ENOUGH FOR MY TEACHER TO APPROVE OF ME.

I WON'T HAVE A GOOD LIFE IF MY TEACHER DOESN'T LIKE ME.

HA!

HA!
HA!

HA!

THE TRUTH

KEY VERSE

Titus 3:1 (ESV)

"Remind them to be submissive to rulers and authorities, to be obedient, to be ready for every good work, to speak evil of no one, to avoid quarreling, to be gentle, and to show perfect courtesy toward all people."

Have you ever thought, "Why is my teacher hard on me?" One reason could be because of the potential they see in you. Like a good sports coach who trains his athletes hard, your teacher is training you to draw out the greatness in you.

It's always our choice how we respond to people who appear to treat us unfairly. David is an amazing example of this. He served King Saul faithfully even though King Saul tried to kill him! David had a chance to get revenge more than once. However, David knew what pleased his Heavenly Father and never spoke badly against King Saul.

Everyone has different personalities, including teachers. Some people are easier to connect with than others. But that does not mean that we can't learn from those who are hard to connect with, or that we can't show them respect and love. Your attitude toward your teacher will determine how much you will grow during the time that he or she is your teacher.

WHAT CAN I SAY?

- My teacher wants me to succeed.
- My hunger to learn helps me keep a good attitude.
- I treat others how I want to be treated, no matter what.
- I will succeed no matter what kind of teacher I have.

WHAT CAN I DO?

- **Be teachable -** Like Jesus, be hungry to learn. As a boy, Jesus loved to sit in the Synagogue to learn and discuss things. Even the Creator of the universe wanted to learn, and the Bible says He grew in favor (Luke 2:52). "Likewise you younger people, submit yourselves to your *elders*. Yes, all of *you* be submissive to one another, and be clothed with humility, for "God opposes the proud, but gives grace to the humble" (1 Peter 5:5).

- **Pull out the gold -** Gold miners have to dig through a lot of dirt to find gold. It can be the same with people, and the gold is so precious! Sift through any "dirt" (things you don't like) that you see in your teacher, and find the gold. Find three things they do well and that you appreciate about them. Now that you see some gold, decide to honor and respect them. "So we don't look at the troubles we can see now; rather, we fix our gaze on things that cannot be seen" (2 Corinthians 4:18).

- **Imagine yourself in their shoes -** It's easy to misunderstand people if you don't know the hard things they have to do. Ask yourself, "Is it easy to look after a classroom full of kids? Is it fun for them to be disrespected by students?" Your teacher has feelings too. Ask yourself, "What can I do to encourage my teacher?" "Getting wisdom is the wisest thing you can do! And whatever else you do, develop good judgment" (Proverbs 4:7).

I CANNOT CHANGE

You've tried really hard all month to change a couple of your bad habits, and you feel like you've failed. You tried to be nicer to your sister, but you ended up saying something mean. You tried to do all your homework on time, but you made a mess of it and turned it in late. You are becoming discouraged, and you feel bad about yourself. "What's the point?" you ask. "I might as well give up trying to change. When I do try, nothing changes anyway." *Beep, beep, beep!* It's the lie alarm! Grab your Laughter Blaster and zap that lie to bits!

LET'S ZAP THESE LIES TO BITS!

GOD'S RESURRECTION POWER ISN'T STRONG ENOUGH TO HELP ME CHANGE.

IT'S EASIER FOR OTHER PEOPLE TO CHANGE THAN IT IS FOR ME.

CHANGING THE WAY I THINK WON'T CHANGE THE WAY I AM.

IF I TRY TO CHANGE, IT WON'T WORK, AND IT'S A WASTE OF MY TIME.

PEOPLE LIKE ME CAN NEVER CHANGE.

HA! HA! HA! HA! HA! HA! HA!

THE TRUTH

Every person can change with God's help. Gideon started as a wimpy guy hiding from his enemies. God sent an angel to Gideon and told him that he was a mighty man of valor. Once he agreed with God, he overcame a whole army with just 300 men!

King David started as just a shepherd boy and became a great king. It would have been easy for him to say that he couldn't become the king because he came from a farming family. Instead, he decided to agree with who God said he was, and he became the ruler of the Israelites.

Lazarus was dead before Jesus came to him. It looked pretty hopeless for him to change, but three words from Jesus changed everything and brought Lazarus back to life! God says that we can do all things with Christ, and that includes changing into more of who He made us to be.

KEY VERSE

Philippians 4:13

"For I can do everything through Christ, who gives me strength."

WHAT CAN I SAY?

- I can change, and I will change.
- Spending time in God's presence helps me to change.
- I am becoming more like Jesus every day.
- God helps me to change, and He is always with me.

WHAT CAN I DO?

- **Get hope -** Your hopelessness about a problem is a bigger problem than the problem. Focus on how big the power of God is and His heart to help you change. As you change the way you think, you will change the way you act (Romans 12:2). "I pray that God, the source of hope, will fill you completely with joy and peace because you trust in Him. Then you will overflow with confident hope through the power of the Holy Spirit" (Romans 15:13).

- **Give it time -** A farmer sows a crop and then gives it time to grow. He doesn't decide that he's a bad farmer if the crop doesn't grow overnight. You have not failed if change doesn't happen quickly. Keep planting good seeds by making good decisions, and give the good seeds time to grow into good habits. "Consider the farmers who patiently wait for the rains in the fall and in the spring. They eagerly look for the valuable harvest to ripen. You, too, must be patient" (James 5:7-8).

- **Never give up! -** Keep working on changing your thinking and your habits. Forgive yourself if you have a bad day, and start again right away. You will make it if you just keep going. Ask a parent or friend to encourage you with the small steps as they see you changing. Never give up! "So let's not get tired of doing what is good. At just the right time we will reap a harvest of blessing if we don't give up" (Galatians 6:9).

NOBODY LIKES ME

Your mom drops you off at John's birthday party. You know the whole class was invited to this party. Unsure about how you will be welcomed, you take a deep breath and walk into the crowded room. You stand there, waiting for someone to come to you, but nothing happens. You can hear your classmates laughing and talking like you don't exist. Running away seems like a good option as the words "Nobody likes me" start ringing in your head. Wait a minute! You need a weapon for this one. You pull out your favorite laughter weapon because it's a *Power Play* and you blow that lie away! *Ha ha!*

CHOOSE YOUR WEAPON. SAY GOODBYE LIES!

OF ALL THE PEOPLE I KNOW, I AM THE LEAST LIKELY TO BE LIKED.

I AM ALONE.

IF ANYONE DOES NOT LIKE ME, THEN I AM A FAILURE AS A PERSON.

IT DOES NOT MATTER TO GOD IF I HAVE GOOD FRIENDS OR NOT.

PEOPLE SPEND TIME WITH ME BECAUSE THEY FEEL BAD FOR ME.

THE TRUTH

You are loved, liked, and cherished. Jesus really likes you and He calls you His friend (John 15:15). And who could be better to have as a friend than Jesus? Also, you do have people who like you, but when you focus on the people who don't seem to like you, you miss seeing the ones who do. The lie that you don't have friends will stop you from seeing the people who do want to be friends with you.

With Jesus inside of us, we become more attractive. The Bible tells us that we get back what we give out (Luke 6:37-38). In other words, if we are kind and act like Jesus, it is more likely that people will be kind back.

It is possible that not everyone will like you. That's true for everyone, and that's okay. Jesus said that the second most important commandment is to love your neighbor as yourself (Matthew 22:37-38). You get to love people regardless of how they respond, and by doing this you will gain friends and change people's lives for the better.

KEY VERSE

Psalm 5:12

"For you bless the godly, O Lord; You surround them with Your shield of love."

WHAT CAN I SAY?

- I have God's favor on my life, and people like me.
- I love being me.
- God loves me.
- I am choosing to be a great friend.

WHAT CAN I DO?

- **Realize that you are not alone** - *Everyone* has experienced this in his or her life. Laugh hard at this lie, and don't let it become part of your thoughts. Instead, think about how much Jesus loves you and how precious you are to Him! He is always with you, whether you feel Him or not. "I will never fail you. I will never abandon you" (Hebrews 13:5).

- **Believe people will like you** - Believe that people want to be your friend even if they don't seem to like you now. Instead of looking for evidence that people don't like you, look for evidence that they do like you. Every time you see proof of this, write it down on a list, and read it often. This will help you believe it. "Jesus grew in wisdom and in stature and in favor with God and all the people" (Luke 2:52).

- **Be the best you can be** - Don't get into foolish talk or actions to gain friends. People who try too hard to get others to like them usually find that people don't like them. When you feel tempted to do something crazy to get attention, picture walking hand in hand with Jesus. Imagine Him speaking great things about you and giving you courage to be kind to others. Then act as a friend to others, no matter what they are doing to you. "Work willingly at whatever you do, as though you were working for the Lord rather than for people" (Colossians 3:23).

I CAN'T DO ANYTHING ABOUT THE UNSEEN REALM AROUND ME

Your friend's mom just dropped you off from practice, and you walk inside your house to discover that something just doesn't feel right. Everything looks normal. The furniture is the same, the pictures on the wall are the same, and your parents seem okay. "What's up?" you ask your parents, hoping to figure out why it feels strange in here. Your parents tell you everything is fine, but now you have a sinking feeling in the pit of your stomach. You don't know if you feel sad, confused, angry, or scared. "I hate it when this happens. It's just icky! I wish I could change the atmosphere around here. It's so hard to be in my home right now, but I just can't do anything about the way it feels." Suddenly you realize that's a hopeless lie, and you flatten it with your Ha Ha Hammer!

NOW FLATTEN THESE LIES TOO!

THE DEVIL IS MORE POWERFUL THAN THE PRESENCE OF GOD.

I AM NOT STRONG ENOUGH TO CHANGE THE UNSEEN REALM.

WHEN IT FEELS BAD AROUND ME, I CAN'T CHANGE HOW IT FEELS.

BEING AFFECTED BY A BAD ATMOSPHERE IS JUST A NORMAL PART OF LIFE.

I FEEL LIKE THIS BECAUSE SOMETHING IS WRONG WITH ME.

HA! HA! HA! HA! HA!

THE TRUTH

Have you ever walked into a room and it just felt yucky? On the surface it doesn't make sense that it feels strange. Everything looks normal on the outside, but something is going on that you can't see with your eyes. Sometimes the opposite happens, too. You can walk into a room and it feels great to be there. The room feels peaceful and you feel safe.

The atmosphere we feel is real - we just can't always see what causes it. That's why it's called the unseen realm. Sometimes because we can't see it, we believe we can't change it. The truth is that you carry Jesus on the inside of you, and His presence is stronger than anything. If you suddenly feel fear and there is no good reason for it, then you just need to ask Jesus, the Prince of Peace, to show up, and the bad feeling has to disappear. In Joshua 1, God tells Joshua that wherever he goes, God will be with him and give him the power to overcome that place. Because Jesus lives inside of you, you have the power to take any atmosphere and change it, wherever you go. You are part of God's plan for bringing peace, kindness, and love to this world.

WHAT CAN I SAY?

- Nothing is more powerful than God in me.
- My words and actions change the unseen realm.
- God loves to change the atmosphere with His presence.
- Wherever I am, I release peace, hope, and love.

WHAT CAN I DO?

- **Worship, worship, worship** - When you worship, you become more aware of God's presence. He is always with you, but you become more aware of Him when you focus on Him and give Him praise. Praise and worship chase fear and other bad things away. You can praise God out loud, or you can worship Him silently by turning your heart toward Him. "Around midnight Paul and Silas were praying and singing hymns to God, and … the chains of every prisoner fell off" (Acts 16:25-26).

- **Speak to the atmosphere** - Your words have power, and you can change the unseen realm by telling what feels "icky" to go away and by inviting the Presence of God to come in. For example, if you are feeling fearful, you can tell fear to leave and invite peace to come. Use your voice to change the atmosphere wherever you are. "Life is in the power of the tongue" (Proverbs 18:21, NKJV)..

- **Do a prophetic act -** "Then Moses raised his hand over the sea, and the Lord opened up a path through the water with a strong east wind. The wind blew all that night, turning the seabed into dry land" (Exodus 14:21). When Moses raised his hand, it was a prophetic act. We can also do prophetic acts. You could write what you want to get rid of on paper and then tear it up. You could quietly stomp your foot under your desk as if you are crushing negativity. Next time you encounter a bad atmosphere, ask the Holy Spirit what He wants you to do.

MAKING GOOD DECISIONS IS HARD FOR ME

After saving up your allowance for four weeks, your mom finally agrees to take you to the store. As you stroll through the aisles, you see something you love. "That's what I'll spend my money on!" But then something else catches your attention, "No, that's what I want!" Then you notice eight other things that you would love to have, and you are paralyzed with indecision. "I don't know what to spend my money on. I don't know what I like the most. I can't make decisions!" Freeze! You realize you do know how to decide things. You *can* do this. It's a silly lie that you can't make good decisions! *Ha ha!* There is only one remedy for this: you grab your Laugh-achine Gun and laugh that lie into pieces!

READY. AIM. HA HA HA! THESE LIES ARE DONE FOR!

I AM A BAD DECISION MAKER.

IF I MAKE A BAD DECISION, IT WILL RUIN MY LIFE.

EVERYONE WILL THINK I AM STUPID IF I DO THE WRONG THING.

IF I DON'T KNOW WHAT TO DO, I SHOULDN'T DO ANYTHING.

PEOPLE WILL BE MAD AT ME IF I DON'T CHOOSE WHAT THEY WOULD CHOOSE.

THE TRUTH

You are a great decision maker. One of the promises God makes in the Bible is: "If you need wisdom, ask and God will give it to you" (James 1:5). Wisdom is the ability to know what to do in every situation. God will help you know what to do in every situation you face.

Gideon was an adult in the Bible who changed a nation. He knew what he needed to do, but he talked with God to be absolutely sure about it. God answered Him, and helped Him have confidence in his decision (Judges 6:36-40). When we are doubting our decisions, we can ask God to help us know if the decision we want to make is right or wrong.

Sometimes we don't hear something as clearly as we might like. If we desire to honor God in our decisions, God won't be scared of you getting an answer wrong. As children of God, we can have faith and trust that Jesus, who lives in us, leads us at all times. We can stop, think through our options, and make our best decision with our minds and wise adults. Then we attach faith to our decision and trust that we made the right one.

WHAT CAN I SAY?

- I am a great decision maker.
- I always know what to do.
- When I make a bad decision, I am still valuable.
- God gives me wisdom to know what to do.

WHAT CAN I DO?

- **Adopt a "can-do" attitude** - Anything is possible. It is important to start believing this at a young age. You can believe it more by saying it more and thinking it more. Practice saying this out loud three times a day: "God is with me, so I will always know what to do. It's entirely possible for me to make great decisions today!" Consider writing this on a notecard beside your bed. "Anything is possible if a person believes" (Mark 9:23).

- **Stomp on fear** - When you feel like you can't do something, it's an opportunities to kick fear in the face. Practicing things you don't think you're good at brings joy to Jesus and helps you grow. If you are asked to make a decision and fear comes, laugh out loud and tell fear to go away. You are a wonderful decision maker! And you can always ask the Holy Spirit, your Helper, for help making decisions. "So humble yourselves before God. Resist the devil, and he will flee from you" (James 4:7).

- **Practice making decisions and ask for advice** - Next time you have a decision to make, list all the choices you have. Write down what makes each choice good (pros) and what makes each choice look like it's not a good idea (cons). Based on this list, choose the decision you plan to make. Then ask someone you trust for advice on your decision. You can even show them your list. "Without wise leadership, a nation falls; there is safety in having many advisers" (Proverbs 11:14).

I AM A FAILURE

As you sit there watching the other kids give their speeches in class, your stomach feels knotted and the palms of your hands feel sweaty. You know your turn to speak is coming soon. You begin to think back over the other times you have had to do this, and the knot tightens and twists. You felt awful, embarrassed, and shameful. Then the floodgates open and other embarrassing moments start to flood your brain. There it is, a big sign in your mind that says, "I am a failure." *Ha ha!* You recognize that it's a big ugly lie. As you start to laugh, your Laughter Boots kick that lie out the door!

LET'S **KICK** THESE LIES OUT TOO!

I'M GOOD AT NOTHING, AND I NEVER WILL BE.

I NEED TO PROTECT MYSELF FROM FAILURES.

IF I PRETEND I DON'T CARE, IT WILL HIDE MY FEAR.

TRYING HARD IS JUST A WASTE OF TIME.

NO ONE ELSE MESSES UP BUT ME.

THE TRUTH

KEY VERSE

Romans 8:37

"...

overwhelming victory is ours through Christ, who loved us."

Who told you that you are a failure? Probably your past. The past likes to say that if you could not succeed the first time, you never will. The truth is, just because you made a mistake yesterday does not mean anything about you and who you are. You are a success because God says you are (Romans 8:37)! There may be things that you find really difficult to do, but if you spent some time thinking about what you can do, it would be impossible to call yourself a failure.

Here are some Bible characters who overcame big failures to do great things for God: Abraham lied about his wife, but still became the father of the nation of Israel. Joseph was so proud that his brothers sold him into slavery, but he later fed all of Egypt during a famine. Peter denied Jesus three times, yet afterward he preached the sermon that started Christianity.

You are a success if you keep trying, not because you are the best at everything. Believe it or not, at one time you couldn't walk because you were a baby. Now walking probably seems easy. The things you are trying now that seem difficult will one day come very easily to you. The key to success is never giving up.

WHAT CAN I SAY?

- I am built for success.
- Fear of failing won't stop me.
- I learn from my failures.
- I love to do new things.

WHAT CAN I DO?

- **Think, ask, and write** - Everyone can do many things well, including you. Make a list of what you are good at. You can do this by asking yourself and others whom you trust. Put the list somewhere you'll see it often. Read it out loud to yourself every day. "Fix your thoughts on what is true, and honorable, and right, and pure, and lovely, and admirable. Think about things that are excellent and worthy of praise" (Philippians 4:8).

- **Read or watch movies about overcomers** - Everyone else's victories in life are like a prophecy for what we can do. Ask an adult to help you find stories about successful people who overcame failure. Here are some examples: Abraham Lincoln, Thomas Edison, and Joseph (Genesis 37:18-36). "The testimony of Jesus is the spirit of prophecy" (Revelation 19:10, NKJV).

- **Practice growth** - Draw a target on a box. Take five steps back. Now throw a ball 20 times and count how many times the ball hits the target. For the next 7 days, throw the ball at least 20 times at the target. Compare the number of times you hit the target on the seventh day with the number from the first day. See how much you have improved. Growth is always possible when you don't give up. "Work willingly at whatever you do, as though you were working for the Lord rather than for people" (Colossians 3:23).

I'M TOO BAD OF A PERSON TO GET TO HEAVEN

"Jesus, please forgive me for the bad thing I just did. I'm sorry, and I will try never to do it again." That feels better. You pick yourself up and walk back to where you came from, feeling a little bit lighter. You spend the day hanging with your friends. It starts out funny, then it gets a little silly, and then … Oh no! I just did the exact same thing I asked Jesus to forgive me for earlier! A terrible feeling drops down on you like a blanket of doom. "Surely Jesus can't forgive me again so soon. I'm too bad of a person to get to Heaven," you think. And that's when you recognize it. *Ha ha!* Destroy that lie with the *Power Play* laughter weapon of your choice!

WHEN I SIN TOO MUCH, GOD SAYS,
"SORRY, I DON'T WANT TO SEE YOU ANYMORE."

BEING GOOD IS WHAT GETS ME INTO HEAVEN.

BECAUSE I FEEL BAD WHEN I SIN,
GOD MUST FEEL THAT WAY ABOUT ME TOO.

I NEED TO PUNISH MYSELF WHEN I DO SOMETHING WRONG.

THE TRUTH

If you believe Jesus paid for your sins on the cross, and declare Him as your Lord (Romans 10:9), then you are going to Heaven. It's guaranteed! There's no doubt. It's official! You are in God's family, and you are always welcome there.

In the Old Testament, we see stories where God seemed angry and even mean, but that happened before Jesus was punished on the cross. All of God's anger was poured out on Jesus on the cross. Jesus took our place for any bad things we have done, and this means *anything*. Jesus took our punishment so God could do what He wanted, and that was to adopt you into His family (Ephesians 1:5). If you believe in Jesus and love Him, you are in the family of God, and there is no argument about that. In fact, He is preparing a mansion in Heaven for you to live in with Him forever (John 14:2)!

If you have never asked Jesus into your heart, go to page 85 for information on how to do that right now.

If you have never asked Jesus into your heart, go to page 85 for information on how to do that right now.

KEY VERSE

Ephesians 2:9

"Salvation is not a reward for the good things we have done, so none of us can boast about it."

WHAT CAN I SAY?

- Jesus paid for all my sins and He gets me into Heaven.
- There is no sin that can keep me from God.
- I am in the family of God, and I am always welcome.
- It is because of the cross that I am saved.

WHAT CAN I DO?

- **Read the promises of God** - Look up one of these Bible verses each day: John 5:24, Romans 10:13, 1 John 5:11-13, Ephesians 2:8-9, Romans 8:1, John 6:37, Romans 10:9, John 10:27-30, Romans 8:16, Acts 2:21, 1 John 3:20, and Romans 8:38-39. If you don't have a Bible, you can look these up online.

- **Stay close to Jesus** - You are a child of God because of what Jesus has done for you. If you do something wrong, clean up your mess, say you're sorry, and then move even closer to Jesus. "... nothing can ever separate us from God's love. Neither death nor life, neither angels nor demons, neither our fears for today nor our worries about tomorrow—not even the powers of hell can separate us from God's love ... nothing in all creation will ever be able to separate us from the love of God that is revealed in Christ Jesus our Lord" (Romans 8:38-39).

- **Talk to someone** - "Confess your sins to each other and pray for each other ..." (James 5:16). This verse says to tell others about your sins. You may think this sounds scary, and at times it can be. But it will bring you freedom when you bring your sins out of darkness and into the light by telling someone who is safe to tell. If you find yourself doing things over and over again that you don't want to do, you need to ask someone to help you. Ask God to help you know who to talk to.

MY OPINION DOESN'T MATTER

Today was the day you finally spoke up in class, and you're not sure anyone listened to what you said. Then you were in a room of adults with your parents and you said something, but it seemed like no one heard you. Inside your head you're hearing, "Your opinion doesn't matter! Your voice isn't important or powerful. No one cares what you have to say." As you feel hopelessness rise within you, you suddenly realize it's not true! It's time to silence this lie. You pull out your Giggle Grenade and blast that lie out of town!

THESE LIES COULD USE A GIGGLE GRENADE TOO!

I AM NOT OLD ENOUGH FOR MY OPINIONS TO BE TAKEN SERIOUSLY.

IF I HAVE AN OPINION DIFFERENT FROM MY PARENTS, I AM PROBABLY JUST BEING REBELLIOUS.

PEOPLE WILL ONLY HEAR ME IF I THROW A TEMPER TANTRUM.

IT IS TOO HARD TO SAY WHAT I MEAN.

HA!

HA!
HA!

HA!

THE TRUTH

KEY VERSE

1 Timothy 4:12

"Don't let anyone think less of you because you are young. Be an example to all believers in what you say, in the way you live, in your love, your faith, and your purity."

You have great ideas and a good mind. Timothy was a young leader in the Bible who was making a difference in the world. Paul encouraged Timothy not to let anyone look down on him, but for Timothy to set an example for other believers in what he said, what he did, how he loved, and how he lived (with faith and purity).

Not only can other kids and adults listen to and learn from you, but even God likes to hear your opinion. In Exodus 32, God had a plan, but Moses shared his opinion with Him. Through a conversation and several of these opinions shared by Moses, God actually changed His plan of action. Moses respected God, but he was not scared to share his opinion with Him. And God listened to Moses ... it's amazing that the King of the universe wants to hear what we think!

WHAT CAN I SAY?

- My opinions matter to God and others.
- Because of my age, I see the world in a special way.
- When I am not heard, I keep a good attitude.
- I am easily able to say what I mean to say.

WHAT CAN I DO?

- **Believe you are special** - Jesus told adults to be like kids (Matthew 18 and Luke 18). As a young person, you see the world differently from adults. You will grow in experience and keep getting smarter, and that is valuable. But remember that having the mind of a child is good for you and adults. "... unless you turn from your sins and become like little children, you will never get into the Kingdom of Heaven" (Matthew 18:3).

- **Stay confident** - When others don't listen to you, it's good to remember that you have the Holy Spirit living inside of you. Even if your voice is not heard, you can still live in a way that is an example. Just like Timothy set an example for a lot of believers, you too can live with love, joy, peace, patience, kindness, goodness, faithfulness, gentleness, and self control. This is because "... the Spirit of God lives in you" (1 Corinthians 3:16).

- **Practice giving your opinion** - When you are asked what you think, do your best to answer. Be honest. Say what you feel and think, and let people ask you more questions. If you need to practice more, try using this question: "Would you like to know what I think?" It is important to remember that even when no one listens to you, you are successful because you are taking risks and learning to use your voice with love and respect. "... give us, your servants, great boldness in preaching Your Word" (Acts 4:29).

I CAN'T OVERCOME FEAR

It's time to go to bed. You heard a great bedtime story, but once the light is turned off and the door is closed, fear starts to creep in. A little noise sounds louder than usual, and you just know the monster under your bed is real. You wish you could turn on the light. You can feel it in the room. You felt this same thing yesterday at the doctor's office. It's like you can't breathe, and you feel like there is nothing you can do to overcome it. Wait a second! The only thing you're facing is fear, and it can be beat. That lie isn't working this time or ever again because you have your Laughter Blaster! *Boom!* You blast that lie to oblivion!

LET'S **BLAST** THESE LIES TO OBLIVION TOO!

FEAR IS TOO POWERFUL.

THERE WILL ALWAYS BE SOMETHING I AM AFRAID OF.

FEAR WILL HOLD ME BACK IN MY LIFE.

BECAUSE I CAN'T OVERCOME FEAR, I HAVE TO LIVE WITH IT.

GOD IS NOT POWERFUL ENOUGH TO HELP ME OVERCOME MY FEAR.

HA! HA! HA! HA! HA! HA!

THE TRUTH

Fear is just a bully. It does not have any power. It just tries to intimidate you. God has overcome all things, including fear (John 16:33). More than 100 times, the Bible says not to be afraid. There are many other words used that have the same meaning. The Bible says not to worry, not to be anxious, and not to fret.

God knows things in life can be scary, like certain animals, storms, nature, and even people. Here is what God gives us to help us deal with fear: His supernatural protection (Psalm 91 and 121), a sound mind (2 Timothy, 1:7 NKJV), and His perfect love (1 John 4:18).

The truth is that He is watching over us, and He has given us authority over all things (Matthew 28:18). He also encourages us that we can do even greater things than Jesus did (John 14:12). To do these greater things, it may sometimes feel scary. But when fear comes at you, you can remember the truth that God is greater in you and that *you can overcome!* And remember, every time you worship, the enemy flees. Worship always brings the Kingdom of God, and the devil can't enter that.

KEY VERSE

2 Timothy 1:7

"For God has not given us a spirit of fear and timidity, but of power, love, and self-discipline."

WHAT CAN I SAY?

- Jesus is bigger and stronger than fear.
- I am an overcomer.
- Fear is nothing but a bully.
- God's perfect love takes away my fear.

WHAT CAN I DO?

- **Decide to be brave -** Everyone battles with fear, but you can overcome it. Think about everyone you know who is brave. They can be storybook heroes, Bible characters, or people you know. Imagine yourself, like them, overcoming scary things in life and big challenges. Make a list of fears that you can overcome. Reward yourself each time you overcome something you were afraid of. "For God has not given us a spirit of fear and timidity, but of power, love, and self-discipline" (2 Timothy 1:7).

- **Remember times you've overcome fear already -** David fought and killed a lion and a bear before he killed Goliath (you can read the story in 1 Samuel 17:34-50). Write down three things you were scared of when you were younger that you aren't scared of now. Celebrate these victories and know that God is going to also help you overcome fears you will face in the future.

- **Be a powerful person of love -** Love is very powerful. Sometimes when something frightens you, your parents might be afraid as well. Yet they often protect you and battle whatever it is that scares you in order to keep you safe. They do this because their love for you is so powerful. Next time you're afraid of something, focus on being a powerful person of love and let love help give you the courage and strength you need to overcome the fear. "... perfect love expels all fear" (1 John 4:18).

I'M NOT A GOOD FRIEND

HA! HA! HA! HA! HA! HA! HA!

All the other children seem to have such an easy time making and keeping friends. You, on the other hand, seem to struggle with it. Yesterday you borrowed a toy from your best friend, and you accidently broke it. Today all the kids are sharing snacks, and you don't have anything good to offer. "They all get along so well," you think to yourself. "Why can't it be that easy for me?! I'm not a good friend." Hey, what's that funny smell in the air? It's a stinky lie! You pull out your Ha Ha Hammer and *SMASH* this lie, and a big gust of wind comes and blows it away!

SMASH, SMASH, SMASH! BYE BYE LIES!

I DON'T KNOW HOW TO BE A GOOD FRIEND TO SOMEONE.

THERE IS NO REASON PEOPLE WOULD WANT TO BE MY FRIEND.

I DON'T DESERVE TO HAVE FRIENDS.

THERE IS NOTHING I CAN DO TO BECOME A BETTER FRIEND.

HA! HA! HA! HA! HA!

THE TRUTH

KEY VERSE

Luke 6:31

"Do to others as you would like them to do to you."

Sometimes it can seem hard to make and keep friends. Friendship is a learned skill, and we can grow in it. As we decide to learn new skills, we have an incredible helper - the Holy Spirit. The Holy Spirit is our teacher, and He teaches us how to be a good friend (John 14:26) and how to love like God loves. God asks us to be loving and gives us the power to be loving. 1 Corinthians 13:4-7 talks about what love looks like. Loving others is being patient, kind, and humble. God doesn't ask us to do things that are impossible for us. He only asks us to do things we can do.

Also, God is your friend. John 15:15 says that He calls us His friend. This is amazing! God, who created the universe, is friends with you. You are lovable and likable, and Father God loves you as much as He loves Jesus (John 17:23). God likes you so much that He is celebrating you and singing over you (Zephaniah 3:17). Noticing how God is a good friend to you teaches you how to be a good friend to others.

WHAT CAN I SAY?

- I am a great friend!
- I am a friendly person, and people like to be around me.
- I am growing my friendship skills.
- I am a loving and generous friend.

WHAT CAN I DO?

- **Make a difference** - Ask God which of your friends could use some attention. Make something special for them, and give it to them as a gift. It could be a drawing, a painted rock, a bracelet, or anything else you think they would enjoy. "If you need wisdom, ask our generous God, and he will give it to you" (James 1:5).

- **Grow your friendship skills** - Regularly give compliments to your friends. Smile and say hello to people. Improve your listening skills. Be the first one to be friendly instead of waiting for others to be a friend to you. Be the most encouraging and friendly person you know! "Do to others whatever you would like them to do to you" (Matthew 7:12).

- **Love yourself** - Believe it or not, we can dislike and even hate ourselves. When we have self-hatred, we try to pretend to be something we are not to win friends. When we are pretending, we cannot truly connect with other people. The best way to win friends and have others like you is for you to like yourself and be yourself! A great way to start liking yourself is to learn what God says about you. Search this book for the truth about who you are and learn to like, and love, yourself!

ONE PERSON CANNOT CHANGE THE WORLD

You're watching a movie and the good guy overcomes all the challenges he faces and changes the world. At one point it really looked like the hero couldn't possibly win, but in the end he did win. You think, "Well it always works out for the hero in movies, but it never seems to works out for me. I want to help everyone, but I can't change the world. It's impossible for one person to change the world." Wait a minute! God says nothing is impossible ... it must be a lie that one person cannot change the world. This calls for a *Power Play!* Pick the laughter weapon that you can do the most damage with, and get this lie for good!

IT'S A POWER PLAY! GOT YOUR BEST WEAPON? SAY GOODBYE LIES!

JESUS WAS JOKING WHEN HE SAID WE WOULD DO GREATER THINGS THAN HIM.

I MUST BE PERFECT TO CHANGE THE WORLD.

I'M POWERLESS TO CHANGE THE WORLD.

GOD HAS SELECTED ONLY A FEW SPECIAL PEOPLE TO CHANGE THE WORLD, AND I AM NOT ONE OF THEM.

WHAT DOES GOD SAY?

KEY VERSE

Hebrews 11:12

"And so a whole nation came from this one man who was as good as dead–a nation with so many people that, like the stars in the sky and the sand on the seashore, there is no way to count them."

There are many people in the Bible who changed the world, which shows us it is possible for one person to do it. The people in the Bible who changed the world did it because they listened and responded to God, not because they were someone "extra special."

Esther saved the Jews because she was willing to risk her life in order to follow God. Abraham listened to God many times, and he changed history. Noah heard God, made the ark even before it started raining, and saved mankind (and animals!). David was still young when he spent time with God and learned to hear and respond to His voice. His life still encourages us today, and he's known as the "man after God's own heart" even though he made some big mistakes.

Like these people who changed the world, you too are a world changer.

WHAT CAN I SAY?

- I am a world changer.
- I will do greater things than Jesus did.
- Nothing is impossible for God, and He is always with me.
- I believe what God says about me.

WHAT CAN I DO?

- **Believe truth** - What you believe determines how you will act. Choose to believe what God says about you. "Anything is possible if a person believes" (Mark 9:23). "... with God everything is possible" (Matthew 19:26). Jesus said, "I tell you the truth, anyone who believes in Me will do the same works I have done, and even greater works, because I am going to be with the Father" (John 14:12).

- **Read stories of people who made a difference** - Read how people in the Bible changed the world. Learn about others who did amazing things and changed history. Spend time thinking and praying about how God might use you to bring change to the world. Write down what He tells you. "Such things were written in the Scriptures long ago to teach us. And the Scriptures give us hope and encouragement as we wait patiently for God's promises to be fulfilled" (Romans 15:4).

- **Don't be afraid to start small** - Big accomplishments result from a series of small steps. Ask God to show you a plan to help your school, sports club, or community to be a better place. Practice changing the world by changing small things, then grow from there. "Do not despise these small beginnings, for the Lord rejoices to see the work begin ..." (Zechariah 4:10).

ASKING JESUS INTO YOUR HEART

If you would like to be sure that you have Jesus in your heart, you can pray this:

Jesus, I thank You that You came to earth to pay for the bad things I did. I thank You that You died for me, won the battle over death, and came back to life. I know that as I believe in You, I am made totally clean and acceptable to God. Jesus, I want to do what pleases You. I ask You to come live in my heart. I ask that Your Holy Spirit would fill me and help me believe the way You do. I ask that You help me get to know Papa God and to experience His great love for me. I thank You that, because I believe in You, I now have life in Heaven forever. Amen.

TESTIMONIES

When River (age 6) woke up one morning he said, "Mommy, it works! My truth is stronger than lies." He held up the truth-o-meter man he made in Kid's Church, and said for every lie Satan has, God has truth stronger and crushes the lie. He told me that Satan wanted him to be scared of the dark, but that God was bigger and His truth made him have no more bad dreams! Then River added that Satan was just faking his power, trying to make him scared. Haha.

I think I need to make a truth-o-meter man too! I'm thankful for children's ministries that reinforce the truth to our kids and grateful for Steve Backlund and his book *Let's Just Laugh at That For Kids!*

I bought this book (*Let's Just Laugh at That For Kids!*) for myself after a friend recommended it. I love this book! It provides a light-hearted, Bible-centered approach to teaching kids about sneaky lies and the proper truths to combat them. Our kids are 8, 5, and 3, and they all love it. As a mom, I love having the tools to help my kids think about what they're thinking about. My 8 year old can now say to me, "Mom, I think I found a stinky lie I was believing …" and we can start the conversation from there. The book includes profound but easy-to-read examples, corresponding Bible verses, and truths to declare to replace stinky lies. You should get this book. It is fun, insightful, and a great way to teach our kids what matters.

I just wanted to comment to share a little anecdote with you. I bought the first *Let's Just Laugh at That For Kids book* for my 7 grandchildren a while back. My daughter has been using it during their devotion time to teach them. This past Monday, while playing football, a little fella on the opposing team got really mad at my 8-year-old grandson and called him a "really big, meanie head." Without missing a beat, Gentry responded "Well, I don't receive that!" and promptly walked away. PRICELESS!! And he learned it from your book. Keep up the awesome work - you are making a huge impact for the Kingdom!

Love this book (*Let's Just Laugh at That For Kids!*) and the ministry of Steve and Wendy Backlund! I'm a homeschooling mom and we're working through this book as a part of our school days. Steve does a great job of highlighting lies that kids of any age can get sucked into believing and operating out of. I love the principle of "let's just laugh at that" in that it helps us all to be aware of our thoughts and that we don't have to accept everything that goes through our minds as truth. We have to manage our minds and our thoughts and it makes dealing with it spiritually not "over spiritual" or serious. While there's a place for rebuking lies and such, I love teaching my kids to identify thoughts and then to laugh at lies and focus on Jesus and TRUTH! If we're speaking out truth we can't at the same time be thinking lies - that's something that would have been revolutionary to learn and practice as a child rather than learning it in my 30's.

MY DAILY DECLARATIONS

Declarations help us build our faith! When we believe them, we will be ready to receive even more of God's goodness!

1. My prayers are powerful!

2. God loves to provide for me.

3. I am free from sin and alive in Him.

4. My health gets better every day.

5. God has supernatural protection for me.

6. I am great at relationships.

7. Because God is with me, the people around me experience His love and power.

8. Because of Jesus, I am loved 100% and super blessed.

9. My family is blessed.

10. I recognize and laugh at the devil's lies.

Hearing truth helps us grow in faith. We must have faith to believe God's promises when negative things feel and sound true. We say declarations out loud to grow our faith.

1. My words direct my life.

2. God is on my side. I can't be beaten!

3. I am a leader, I have great ideas, and God makes me powerful.

4. When I speak truth, my faith grows and I become who God made me to be.

5. I think right thoughts, I speak words of life, and I make good decisions even when it is tough.

6. God will use me today to release His power and love to the people around me.

7. Today will be the best day yet!

To move mountains with Jesus, we need to speak to things. Let's say these!

1. Because I love Jesus, angels are working for me.

2. Bad things are turned away from me because of Jesus' protection.

3. I am a person of peace and bring peace to those around me.

4. I tell stress, sadness, and lack to leave in Jesus' name.

5. This day is a blessed day. I can't wait to see how God's goodness shows up!

POWERFUL PHRASES FOR PARENTS

1) "WHO TOLD YOU THAT?"

Many times, our past is speaking things to us that are not true. When we hear phrases that cause hopelessness about our future, we have to ask ourselves, "Who told you that?" If Jesus told you, through the Bible or by speaking it directly to you, you can trust it is the truth. If you learned to believe it another way and it isn't what God says, then it's a lie. If what you believe isn't what you would encourage your friend with, and if it doesn't bring hope, then it is a lie.

2) "WHAT DOES GOD'S WORD SAY?"

Just because something feels true does not make it the truth. Sometimes kids feel like friends don't like them because they didn't smile at them. It feels like they stopped being friends, but the truth is that they are just having a bad day because their dog died or someone yelled at them. Lies can often feel really true, especially when we have believed them for a long time. When we become great lie detectives, we know that feelings don't make something true. The Word of God is the truth that we can live our lives by.

3) "THE JOY OF THE LORD IS MY STRENGTH!"

No one can steal our joy. It comes from God, and He gives it freely to us. Joy is God's way of giving us strength. There are always going to be hard days. The good news is that we get to choose how we respond to them. When we choose joy, strength is released to us to deal with the hard times. We get to choose to be joyful.

4) "THERE IS ALWAYS A SOLUTION."

Sometimes, especially as a child, it seems like there is no way out of a hard situation. No matter what we try to do, nothing seems to change. The truth is that there is always a way through it. Luke 1:37 says that nothing is impossible with God. When we choose to believe that there is a solution, we are prepared to find that solution with God.

5) "CELEBRATE PROGRESS, NOT PERFECTION."

There is always something to celebrate. While we are still on a journey, celebrating our growth is a key tool in defeating the enemy's lies. Look intentionally for areas where you have already grown. The goal in fighting lies is not to be perfect, but to keep growing.

ADDITIONAL IGNITING HOPE RESOURCES

LET'S JUST LAUGH AT THAT
BY STEVE BACKLUND

Our hope level is an indicator of whether we are believing truth or lies. Truth creates hope and freedom, but believing lies brings hopelessness and restriction. We can have great theology but still be powerless because of deception about the key issues of life. Many of these self-defeating mindsets exist in our subconscious and have never been identified. This book exposes numerous falsehoods and reveals truth that makes us free. Get ready for a joy-infused adventure into hope-filled living.

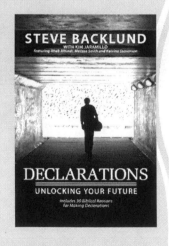

DECLARATIONS
BY STEVE BACKLUND

"Nothing happens in the Kingdom unless a declaration is made." Believers everywhere are realizing the power of declarations to empower their lives. *Declarations* shares 30 biblical reasons for declaring truth over every area of life. Steve Backlund and his team also answer common objections and concerns to the teaching about declarations. The revelation this book carries will help you to set the direction your life will go. Get ready for 30 days of powerful devotions and declarations that will convince you that life is truly in the power of the tongue.

Find more resources including books, group studies, and declarations lists at *ignitinghope.com*

ADDITIONAL RESOURCES

KINGDOM TOOLS FOR TEACHING
BY JANINE MASON

The Creator of the universe has His eye on the education systems of the world and, in particular, on your classroom. He longs to have His presence expressed in every school across the globe, influencing faculty and students alike. His presence in schools is not illegal though mentioning His name may be. *Kingdom Tools for Teaching; Heavenly Strategies for Real Classrooms* brings inspiration and practical tools to empower and activate teachers in bringing the Kingdom of God to their classrooms.

Are you ready to change the way you teach?

I DECLARE POSTER

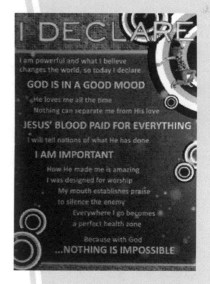

Commonly known as Bethel Church's "Offering Reading #4," this powerful declaration originated in Bethel Church's Children's Ministry! This poster features powerful truths such as "God is in a good mood," "I am important," "Jesus' blood paid for everything," and "nothing is impossible." At 18"x 24", this poster is the perfect size to be hung in a child's bedroom or a children's ministry department. Great for ALL ages, as these truths transcend all ages – children and adults!

For more excellent resources, including curriculum for children's ministry, visit *sethdahl.com*

Made in the USA
Las Vegas, NV
01 August 2022

52510060R00063